Iguanas

By Sandra Donovan

Raintree

ANIMALS OF THE RAINFOREST

www.raintreepublishers.co.uk
Visit our website to find out more information about Raintree books.

To order:
☎ Phone 44 (0) 1865 888112
🖷 Send a fax to 44 (0) 1865 314091
💻 Visit the Raintree Bookshop at www.raintreepublishers.co.uk to browse our catalogue and order online.

First published in Great Britain by Raintree Publishers, Halley Court, Jordan Hill, Oxford, OX2 8EJ, part of Harcourt Education.
Raintree is a registered trademark of Harcourt Education Ltd.

Originated by Dot Gradations
Printed and bound in China by South China Printing

ISBN 1 844 21118 5
07 06 05 04 03
10 9 8 7 6 5 4 3 2 1

British Library Cataloguing in Publication Data
Donovan, Sandra
1. Iguanas – Juvenile literature
2. Rainforest ecology – Junvenile literature
597.9'5
A catalogue for this book is available from the British Library.

Acknowledgements
The publishers would like to thank the following for permission to reproduce photographs:
NHPA, pp. **5, 27**; Root Resources/Earl Kubis, p.**1**; Kenneth Fink, **23–29**; Roving Tortoise Productions/Tui De Roy, pp. **6, 14, 16, 18, 21, 22**; Visuals Unlimited/Ken Lucas, p. **8**; Beth Davidow, pp. **11, 12**; Joe McDonald, pp. **24, 26**.

Cover photograph reproduced with permission of Corbis Royalty Free

Every effort has been made to contact copyright holders of any material reproduced in this book. Any omissions will be rectified in subsequent printings if notice is given to the publishers.

Contents

Any words appearing in the text in bold, **like this**, are explained in the Glossary.

NICARAGUA

Caribbean Sea

COSTA
RICA

PANAMA

VENEZUELA

COLOMBIA

GALAPAGOS
ISLANDS

ECUADOR

Pacific Ocean

Amazon River

BRAZIL

PERU

N
W   E
S

Range of the marine iguana
Surrounding land
Sea
Borders
Rivers

A quick look at iguanas

What do iguanas look like?

Iguanas are lizards. Their bodies can reach up to 2 metres long. They have four short, strong legs. An iguana's tail is usually twice as long as its body. An iguana is usually green, brown, grey, blue or orange and may have stripes or patterns on its skin.

Where do iguanas live?

Iguanas live in warm parts of Central America, South America, the West Indies, the Galapagos Islands, Fiji, Mexico and the south-western part of the USA.

What do iguanas eat?

Iguanas eat soft leaves, flowers and fruit. They get most of their water from their food and lick raindrops from leaves when they are thirsty.

This iguana is eating the last leaves from a rainforest tree branch.

Iguanas in the rainforest

Iguanas are lizards. Lizards are reptiles with four legs. Their long bodies and tails are covered with **scales**. Scales are small, thick, tough pieces of skin. A reptile is a crawling animal with a backbone. Reptiles breathe air and are also **cold-blooded**. The body of a cold-blooded animal warms or cools to about the same temperature as the air or water around it.

The scientific name for iguanas is Iguanidae. This word means 'large lizard' in Spanish.

Iguanas live in warm places like tropical forests and rainforests. A rainforest is a warm place where many different trees and plants grow close together, and a lot of rain falls. Iguanas eat fruits and berries. The seeds pass out of their bodies in their waste, or droppings. Many of these seeds grow into new plants.

This iguana is resting on a tree in the rainforest where it lives.

Where do iguanas live?

Wild iguanas live only in warm parts of the world. Rainforest iguanas like the tropical forests of Central America, South America, Mexico, the West Indies, Fiji and the Galapagos Islands.

Different kinds of iguanas are found in different **habitats**. A habitat is a place where an animal or plant usually lives or grows. Many iguanas live in hot, wet rainforests, deserts or dry tropical forests. Others live around the ocean.

Most iguanas are **arboreal**. This means they live in trees. Iguanas are very good climbers. They spend much of their time about 18 to 20 metres above ground in the **canopy**. The canopy is the area of thick leaves and branches high above the rainforest floor.

The canopy provides a place for iguanas to hide from predators. Predators are animals that hunt other animals and eat them. Iguanas are usually green, grey, brown, blue or orange. Some have stripes or patterns on their skin. Their normal colour **camouflages** them in the trees. Camouflage is colours and patterns that help an animal blend in with the things around it.

Iguanas are good swimmers and usually live near water. Those that do not live by oceans make their homes by rivers and streams.

Many iguanas live in areas where there are other iguanas. Each iguana has its own **territory**. It lives and looks for food in its territory. Iguanas will often defend their territories against other iguanas.

Types of iguana

There are about 30 **species** of true iguana. A species is a group of animals or plants that share common features and are closely related to each other. Iguanas live in a variety of habitats.

The common iguana, or green iguana, lives in the rainforests of Central America and South America. It is the largest iguana. It can grow to be more than 180 centimetres long. Its skin is green and grey.

Two species of iguanas live on the Galapagos Islands, off the coast of Ecuador in the Pacific Ocean. The Galapagos land iguana grows to be about 90 centimetres long. It is green, brown and black.

The Galapagos marine iguana lives in the water around the islands. This green and brown iguana can be over one metre long. It is the only species of lizard that can eat under water.

 This is a male common iguana.

The Fiji iguana is a rare type of iguana. It is found only on the islands of Fiji and Tongo in the Pacific Ocean. Fiji iguanas live mostly in rainforest trees. They are green with white spots or with blue or white stripes. Some have yellow nostrils. They can grow to be about 60 centimetres long.

You can see the dewlap hanging from this iguana's neck.

What do iguanas look like?

Iguanas come in different sizes but most look very similar. They all have scaly skin. Scales are made of a material called keratin. People's fingernails are also made of keratin. An iguana's scales keep moisture and heat within its body.

Some iguanas have a row of spiky scales down their backs or tails, or under their chins.

Iguanas may have a dewlap too. Dewlaps are pieces of coloured skin under their throats. Males use their dewlaps to attract mates. They also use them to appear larger in order to scare away enemies, such as wild dogs, cats and larger iguanas.

Iguanas have three eyes. They have one eye on each side of their heads. The third eye is on top of their heads. This eye cannot be seen from the outside. Scientists think iguanas can see only light and dark with this third eye.

Iguanas all have long bodies with four short, strong legs. Iguanas have five toes on each foot. The toes have long, sharp claws at the end. Iguanas use these claws to dig and to climb trees quickly.

An iguana's tail is usually twice as long as the rest of its body. An iguana's tail has many uses. Rainforest iguanas use their tails as weapons. They lash them at their enemies. They also use their tails to balance when they run. Iguanas swish their tails back and forth to swim.

This land iguana is eating a flower.

What iguanas eat

Most wild iguanas eat flowers, leaves and soft fruits. They are herbivores. A herbivore is an animal that eats only plants.

Adult common iguanas of the rainforest eat fruit, berries and leaves. Young common iguanas may eat insects too. The protein from the insects helps them grow. Marine iguanas eat seaweed that they find on rocks at the edge of the ocean.

Rainforest iguanas do not have to travel far to find food. They eat leaves and fruit from the trees they live in. They also gather food on the rainforest floor. They have good senses of smell and sight, which help them to find food.

Iguanas get their water from the moist food they eat. They also lick drops of rain from leaves.

This marine iguana is eating seaweed off a rock under water.

Eating and digesting food

Once iguanas find their food, they use their long toes and claws to gather it. They bite and grind the food with their sharp teeth.

Iguanas sit in the sun after they have eaten. The warmth of the sun helps them **digest** their food. Digest means to break down food inside the stomach so the body can use it. The bodies of cold-blooded animals have more energy to digest food when they are warmer.

Sometimes it is easy for iguanas to find fruit to eat. This is because of **mast fruiting**. Mast fruiting happens when many trees in a large area produce a lot of fruit at the same time. This happens about every three to seven years. During this time, iguanas eat a lot of fruit. Their bodies turn the extra fruit into fat and store it under their jaws and in their necks.

After mast fruiting, there are many months when it is hard to find fruit. During this time, iguanas eat leaves and live off their stored fat.

Marine iguanas eat seaweed from the ocean floor. They can hold their breath for up to an hour. This means that they can dive, find food and eat under water before coming up for air.

These male iguanas are about to fight each other.

An iguana's life cycle

Iguanas mate at different times of the year. In the rainforest, most iguanas mate just before the rainy season. The rainy season is a period of several months when it rains almost every day. Usually the rainy season is during autumn or spring.

Males and females may become a brighter colour during the mating season. This shows other iguanas that they are ready to mate.

When a male iguana wants to mate with a female iguana, he may raise his dewlap. This tells other males to keep away. A male may charge at another male if he comes too close.

Male iguanas often fight with each other when they both want to mate with the same female. They may scratch, bite or hit each other with their tails until one of them runs away.

Eggs and young

After a male and female iguana have mated, the female often lies in the sun for a long time. This warms the eggs inside her. The female carries her eggs for up to two months.

She will then look for some soft ground in a sunny spot where she can lay her eggs. The eggs need the sun to warm them so they will develop. It is often hard to find a good spot because many areas do not receive enough sun. When this happens, female iguanas may fight each other for good places to lay their eggs.

Before laying eggs, the female digs a hole in the ground with her claws and nose. She lays her eggs in the hole. A female iguana lays up to 50 eggs at a time.

After laying the eggs, the female covers them with soil. The soil helps to protect the eggs from other animals. Sometimes the mother digs several holes to confuse animals looking for eggs to eat. Once the female iguana has covered her eggs with soil, she leaves them. Like many other reptiles, adult iguanas do not take care of their young.

The eggs hatch in eight to ten weeks. Newly hatched iguanas are less than 30 centimetres long.

These young iguanas are climbing on an adult.

Young iguanas look like small adult iguanas.

Iguanas never stop growing. They shed their skin as their bodies grow larger. Iguanas shed their skin in small pieces, instead of in one large piece like snakes.

Wild iguanas live for ten to fifteen years. Iguanas in zoos may live for up to twenty years.

This iguana is opening its mouth to scare off predators.

Surviving in the rainforest

Young iguanas are in danger from predators. Many larger animals of the rainforest eat young iguanas if they can catch them. Young green iguanas are usually bright green. Their colour camouflages them in the trees. As the iguanas get older, their bright green colour often changes to a greyish green or brown. But their bellies usually stay bright green.

Iguanas do different things to scare off their predators, such as birds and larger lizards. They open their mouths to show their teeth. They may hiss and puff up their bodies. They bob their heads up and down and swish their tails back and forth. Sometimes they raise their front legs to make themselves look larger. If they look larger, there is a better chance that smaller animals will be afraid of them.

Young iguanas live low down in the canopy, where the leaves grow close together. It is easier for the iguanas to hide there than higher up.

Adult iguanas live higher in the canopy, where it is sunnier. There are good spots in the canopy for basking. Bask means to lie under a heat source to raise the body temperature. Adult iguanas sometimes fight each other for the best places to bask.

When they begin their day, iguanas leave their sleeping places and move to a basking site. They lie in the sun for several hours. When they are warm, they climb trees and look for food. Then they bask again, while they digest their food. When night comes, they return to their sleeping places.

This green iguana is resting in water in the rainforest.

The future of iguanas

Like many wild animals, iguanas are losing their habitats. The rainforests of Central America are disappearing. People are cutting down trees to make room for new homes and farms. They are also selling the wood from trees. Iguanas in these areas cannot survive without the forests.

Iguanas are also the most popular pet lizards in the world today. Traders buy wild iguanas and sell them as pets. Iguanas need a lot of special attention. Many people do not know how to take care of them. When taken from the wild, iguanas may become ill or die. That is because they need a certain amount of sun, and need to live in certain temperatures. It is hard for people to create the conditions iguanas need in order to survive.

This green iguana is basking in a tree.

Iguanas can lose their tails and grow new ones. Sometimes an iguana's tail is broken off by a predator. When the new tail grows back, it is usually shorter than the old tail. Most lizards can grow a new tail.

What will happen to iguanas?

Some people are raising iguanas on farms. These iguanas are then sold as pets or as food. This means wild iguanas are not taken from the rainforest to be sold as pets.

Some countries are trying to save iguanas. They have made laws against catching and selling iguanas as pets. Without laws, the sale and removal of iguanas from their habitat would probably increase.

Laws are not enough. People must make sure that the laws are obeyed. They must report people who break the laws. They must teach other people about the importance of iguanas. Laws and education may help people keep iguanas alive in their rainforest homes for a very long time.

head
see page 13

eyes
see page 13

dewlap
see page 13

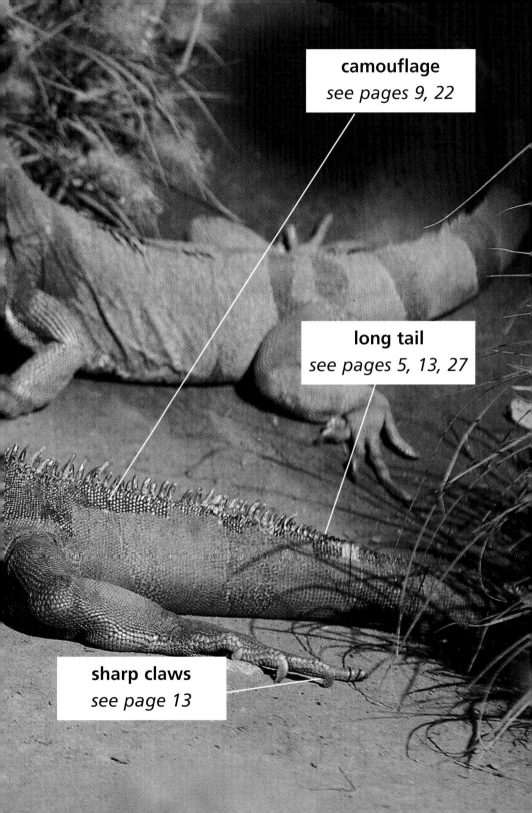

camouflage
see pages 9, 22

long tail
see pages 5, 13, 27

sharp claws
see page 13

Glossary

arboreal living mainly in trees

camouflage colours, shapes and patterns that help an animal or plant blend in with the things around it

canopy thick area of leaves high up in the treetops

cold-blooded animal whose body temperature changes according to its surroundings

digest to break down food so the body can use it

habitat place where an animal or plant usually lives

mast fruiting when many trees in a large area produce a lot of fruit at the same time

scale small piece of thick, hard skin

species group of animals or plants most closely related to each other

territory area in which an animal lives, and which it will fight to keep

Internet sites

Rainforest Concern
www.rainforestconcern.org

World Wide Fund for Nature (WWF)
www.panda.org

Useful address

WWF – UK
Panda House, Weyside Park
Godalming, Surrey
GU7 1XR

Book to read

Theodorou, R; Telford, C. *Amazing Journeys: Up a Rainforest Tree*. Heinemann Library, Oxford, 1998.

Index